D0762270

# RELIGIONS AROUND THE WORLD

# Hinduism

## Katy Gerner

**Marshall Cavendish**
Benchmark

New York

This edition first published in 2009 in the United States of America by Marshall Cavendish Benchmark.

Marshall Cavendish Benchmark
99 White Plains Road
Tarrytown, NY 10591
www.marshallcavendish.us

All Internet sites were available and accurate when sent to press.

First published in 2008 by
MACMILLAN EDUCATION AUSTRALIA PTY LTD
15–19 Claremont Street, South Yarra 3141

Visit our website at www.macmillan.com.au or go directly to www.macmillanlibrary.com.au

Associated companies and representatives throughout the world.

Copyright © Katy Gerner 2008

Library of Congress Cataloging-in-Publication Data

Gerner, Katy.
  Hinduism / by Katy Gerner.
    p. cm. — (Religions around the world)
  Includes index.
  ISBN 978-0-7614-3166-4
  1. Hinduism—Juvenile literature.  I. Title.
  BL1203.G515 2008
  294.5—dc22
                          2008002825

Edited by Erin Richards
Text and cover design by Cristina Neri, Canary Graphic Design
Photo research by Legend Images
Illustrations on pp. 7 and 14 by Andy Craig and Nives Porcellato
Map courtesy of Geo Atlas; modified by Raul Diche

Printed in the United States

## Acknowledgments

The author would like to thank Pundit Narenda Shukla for his suggestions, his wisdom and his time spent reviewing this book.

The author and the publisher are grateful to the following for permission to reproduce copyright material:

Front cover photograph (main): Hindu men carry a large clay idol of Ganesha into the water in Bombay, India © Rob Elliott/AFP/ Getty Images. Other images: book background © Felix Möckel/iStockphoto; OM symbol © Stelian Ion/123RF; Shiva © Michal Rozanski/iStockphoto; Hindu Temple © Patrick Laverdant/iStockphoto; Krishna © Ashwin Kharidehal Abhirama/iStockphoto.

Photos courtesy of: © Stelian Ion/123RF, 5 (top), 22 (top); © World Religions Photo Library/Alamy, 15 (top), 23; Painting by Atul Bose, courtesy www.kamat.com, 18 (left); © Roman Soumar/CORBIS, 28; Dinodia Photo Library, 12 (bottom), 13 (bottom); © Thefinalmiracle/Dreamstime, 27 (right); Rob Elliott/AFP/Getty Images, 16; Asif Hassan/AFP/Getty Images, 17 (left); Sajjad Hussain/ AFP/Getty Images, 5 (bottom); Indranil Mukherjee/AFP/Getty Images, 29 (bottom); Dibyangshu Sarkar/AFP/Getty Images, 21 (top); Noah Seelam/AFP/Getty Images, 7 (right); Prakash Singh/AFP/Getty Images, 8; Zubin Shroff/Stone+/Getty Images, 26; Mansell/Time Life Pictures/Getty Images, 19 (right); Robert Nickelsberg/Time Life Pictures/Getty Images, 25 (top); © Ashwin Kharidehal Abhirama/ iStockphoto, 3 (center); © Robert Bremec/iStockphoto, 9; © cyrop/iStockphoto, 22 (bottom); © Aman Khan/iStockphoto, 4 (bottom center left); © Vasko Miokovic/iStockphoto, 4 (center), 30 (top right); © ngirish/iStockphoto, 14 (top); © Owusu-Ansah/iStockphoto, 4 (bottom center right); © Michal Rozanski/iStockphoto, 1 (left), 31; © Richard Stamper/iStockphoto, 4 (bottom right); © Bob Thomas/iStockphoto, 4 (bottom left); © Alan Tobey/iStockphoto, 32; NASA Goddard Space Flight Center, 4 (center behind); Pelusey Photography, 20 (top left, top right); Photo-Easy.com, 15 (bottom); © Hemis/Alamy/Photolibrary, 10 ; © Kharidehal Abhirama Ashwin/Shutterstock, 3 (bottom), 20 (bottom), 21 (bottom) ; © Andrey Plis/Shutterstock, 11 (bottom); © Vishal Shah/Shutterstock, 6 (bottom), 24; © Gordon Swanson/Shutterstock, 4 (top).

Photos used in book design: book background © Felix Möckel/iStockphoto, 12, 14, 19 ; Hindu Temple © Patrick Laverdant/ iStockphoto, 1, 3, 6, 11, 22, 25, 27, 29, 30; OM symbol © Stelian Ion/123RF, 17; parchment background © Andrey Zyk/iStockphoto, 12, 13, 18, 19.

While every care has been taken to trace and acknowledge copyright, the publisher tenders their apologies for any accidental infringement where copyright has proved untraceable. Where the attempt has been unsuccessful, the publisher welcomes information that would redress the situation.

*For Pem, Penny, Sharpie, Jill and all my in-laws*

1 3 5 6 4 2

# Contents

Glossary words

When a word is printed in **bold**,
you can look up its meaning in the
Glossary on page 31.

# World Religions

Religion is a belief in a supernatural power that must be loved, worshipped, and obeyed. A world religion is a religion that is practiced throughout the world. The five core world religions are Christianity, Islam, Hinduism, Buddhism and Judaism.

People practicing a religion follow practices that they believe are pleasing to their god or gods. Followers read sacred **scriptures** and may worship either privately at home or in a place of worship. They often carry out special rituals, such as when a baby is born, a couple gets married, or someone dies. Religious people have beliefs about how they should behave in this life, and also about life after death.

Learning about world religions can help us to understand each other's differences. We learn about the different ways people try to lead good lives and make the world a better place.

World religions are practiced by many people of different cultures.

# Hinduism

Hinduism is at least five thousand years old. It is the oldest religion still practiced today. Hinduism began in India and is still India's main religion.

Hindus believe that people are **reincarnated** after they die. They can be reborn as any species depending on their actions in their previous life. Humans are considered the most superior of all the species.

Hindus believe the way they behave in this life will affect the way they live in the next. The aim of Hinduism is to lead such a good life that they can escape the cycle of reincarnation and go to heaven. Some believe that they become one with **Brahman**, a powerful form of energy that is everywhere and has always existed.

One Hindu's **faith** can be quite different from another's. This may include the god or goddess they pray to and which scriptures they read. Many Hindus believe in the caste system, which divides Hindus into different groups, or castes. However, the caste system is fading away with time and it is illegal to discriminate against any group.

Under the caste system, Dalit people, the Untouchables, are considered lower than the four castes.

| Hindu caste system | |
|---|---|
| Caste | Traditional roles in society |
| Brahmin | priests and teachers |
| Kshatriya | warriors and rulers |
| Vaisya | shopkeepers, farmers and tradespeople |
| Sudra | servants and laborers |
| Dalit (Untouchables) | the most unpleasant jobs, such as tending **funeral pyres** |

# Religious Beliefs

*H*indus may believe in one or several gods or goddesses. Some believe that the gods are all part of one absolute power, Brahman.

## Gods and Goddesses

The three main gods Indian Hindus worship are:

- Brahma, who created the world (Brahma is not the same as Brahman)
- Vishnu, who takes care of the world
- Shiva, who is also called the destroyer.

Each god has a wife and Shiva has two children. Hindus believe Vishnu appeared on Earth several times to save the world from demons, natural disasters, and cruel people. Vishnu can also help Hindus escape from being born over and over again. Shiva is the destroyer of evil things. Vishnu and Shiva are the most popular gods.

Some Hindus also worship goddesses. Popular goddesses include:

- Saraswati, the goddess of knowledge, art, and education
- Parvati, the goddess of might, wife of Shiva, considered to be extremely beautiful
- Lakshmi, the goddess of wealth, light, wisdom, luck, and beauty.

Statues of Parvati, Shiva, and their two children (left and right).

## Brahman

Brahman is said to be an energy that is everywhere. It is also described as a spirit from which everything has come and which is within everyone. Meditating and doing yoga is believed to help a person realize their unity with Brahman and escape the "bonds of this world."

The philosopher Shankara taught that a person should aim to become part of Brahman when they die. This is to escape the endless cycle of reincarnation and is the ultimate reward for being a good and holy person.

## Mahavakyas

Mahavakyas are "great sayings" of the Upanishads religious texts. They teach about Brahman. They are:

1   Consciousness is Brahman

2   This Self is Brahman

3   Thou art that

4   I am Brahman.

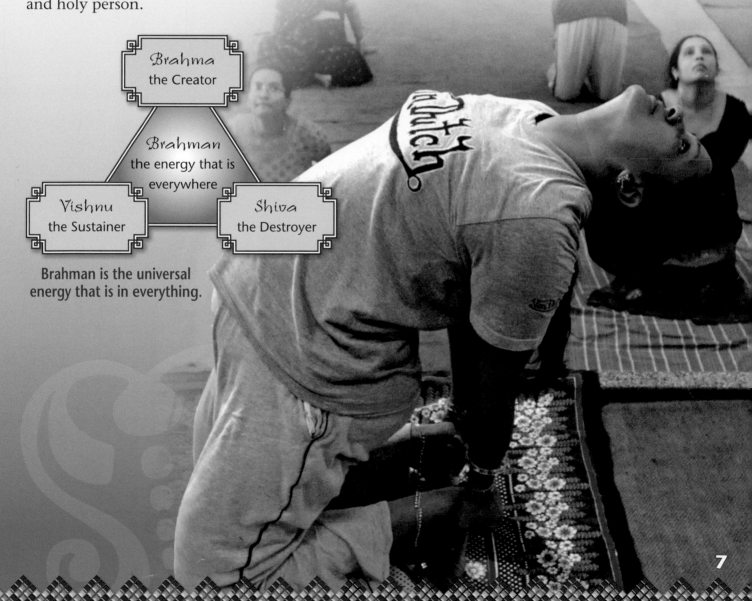

Yoga originated in India and is believed to help with spirituality.

**Brahma**
the Creator

**Brahman**
the energy that is everywhere

**Vishnu**
the Sustainer

**Shiva**
the Destroyer

Brahman is the universal energy that is in everything.

# Beliefs About Behavior

Hindus have strong beliefs about behavior. They believe in **karma** and that all living things are sacred and must be cared for.

## Karma

Hindus believe that their actions in this life determine whether their next life will be a good one. This is called karma. If they are good they believe they will come back as a more important person, such as a priest, and have a happy life. If they lead a bad life and do many unkind things, they will be reborn as a lower species, such as a cockroach.

## Behavior Toward People

Hindus believe that everyone's needs can be met if everyone performs specific duties. These duties include:

- taking care of holy people, the elderly, children, and animals
- protecting the safety of all people
- providing for their extended family
- giving money, food, and clothes that they can spare to people who need them.

Hindus must be honest, kind, and fair. They cannot be greedy and must avoid violence.

A man assists his elderly father after bathing in the holy river Ganges in Varanasi, India.

Cows are sacred animals to Hindus.

## Behavior Toward Animals and Plants

Hindus believe that all living things are sacred. This means animals and plants must be cared for in a responsible and respectful way. Hindus must practice non-violence to all living beings. Most Hindus are vegetarians for this reason.

### Cows

Hindus pray daily for cows. They believe that when cows are cared for properly, every living creature will experience happiness and peace.

### Trees

Planting trees is an important religious duty for Hindus. Trees that can be used for medicines and food are especially important.

## Behavior Toward the Environment

Hindus believe in living a simple life and not using up all the Earth's resources. Hindus should not use oil, coal, or wood at a greater rate than they can be replaced. They also believe that polluting the environment is a bad thing to do.

# Scriptures

There are several scriptures important to Hinduism. Two of the most important are the Vedas and the Bhagavad-gita.

## The Vedas

The Vedas are the oldest scriptures in Hinduism. They were originally passed down **orally** from person to person. They were finally written down between 1500 and 500 BCE. There are four texts in the Vedas.

The Vedas include:

- hymns to the different gods
- information on how to perform rituals properly
- advice for people who withdraw from everyday life to live in the forests
- wise words and sayings
- information on science and music.

Hindus believe that the material in the Vedas is sacred. They also believe the sounds of the words in the Vedas are sacred. The sounds are sacred because they were created by the gods.

A Hindu man studies the sacred scriptures.

# The Bhagavad-gita

The Bhagavad-gita tells the story of the time the god, Krishna, appeared to a warrior named Arjuna. Arjuna did not want to go to war against his friends and relatives. Krishna was his charioteer and offered Arjuna comfort and advice.

Hindus believe that the Bhagavad-gita gives advice on how to behave and act when faced with social and cultural problems. It helps people deal with the battle that goes on inside them when faced with a dilemma.

Some of the things the Bhagavad-gita teaches are:

- to love everybody
- to share everything you own with other people
- to have positive thoughts and let Brahman dwell in your heart
- to aim to achieve self-control
- to be gentle and forgiving with yourself.

The Bhagavad-gita was written in poetry in an ancient language called Sanskrit. It is eighteen chapters long and at least 2,000 years old.

Krishna was Arjuna's charioteer and offered him advice.

# Religious Leaders

Two of the most important Hindu leaders in history are Adi Shankara and Ramanuja.

## Adi Shankara   788–820 CE

Adi Shankara was born in India around 788 CE. He became a Sannyasi, which is a person who gives up material possessions to spend all their time meditating and studying Hinduism. Shankara was famous for his writings and teachings. He studied the Hindu scriptures thoroughly and wrote about them so people could understand them better.

Shankara traveled all around India to teach what he had learned. He liked to write hymns and debate ideas with other people. He started many religious centers, temples, schools, and communities.

Shankara taught that the world we live in is not real. He taught that we should all aim to become part of Brahman, the Supreme Power, when we die. Shankara believed the best way to achieve this is by meditating.

Shankara's writings are very popular and influence many Hindus to this day.

> Brahman is the only truth, the world is unreal, and there is ultimately no difference between Brahman and individual self.
>
> ADI SHANKARA

Kedarnath Temple near the Himalayas in India is a place of pilgrimage to Adi Shankara.

Shankara helped to spread Hinduism throughout India.

# Ramanuja    1017–1137 CE

Ramanuja was born in 1017 CE. He was a very important religious teacher who disagreed with many of Shankara's teachings. Some Hindus felt that Ramanuja's teachings were easier to live by than Shankara's.

Ramanuja taught that loving the god Vishnu and doing good deeds is just as important as meditation. He also believed that people and the world are real, and to say that they are not is an insult to Brahma, the creator.

Ramanuja taught that Vishnu is the most important god. He said that if Hindus spend their whole life worshipping Vishnu and doing what he wants, they will achieve **moksha** when they die. Otherwise they will be born over and over again, until they love and obey Vishnu.

Ramanuja's teachings about loving a particular god became part of what is called the Bhakti movement. Many Hindus still follow the Bhakti movement today.

Ramanuja believed in being devoted to one particular god.

# Worship Practices

May Hindus worship both at a temple and at home. Hindus also believe in going on **pilgrimages**.

## Worshipping at a Temple

Hindus believe that a temple is a living place where Hindus can pray and talk to each other. Priests, who live at the temple, ring bells to let the gods know the worshippers are ready. The worshippers then chant **mantras**, usually for peace. The priests perform a number of religious tasks. They pray, perform rituals, and take care of the temple and the statues of the gods.

Hindus must take off their shoes before they go inside a temple and leave them outside. They also take their shoes off before they go into a wedding altar.

> May all possess happiness. May all be healthy. May all see beauty. May there be good fortune and no misery anywhere. May there be peace everywhere.
>
> VEDIC CHANTS, SAI DARSHAN

This is the typical floor plan of a Hindu temple.

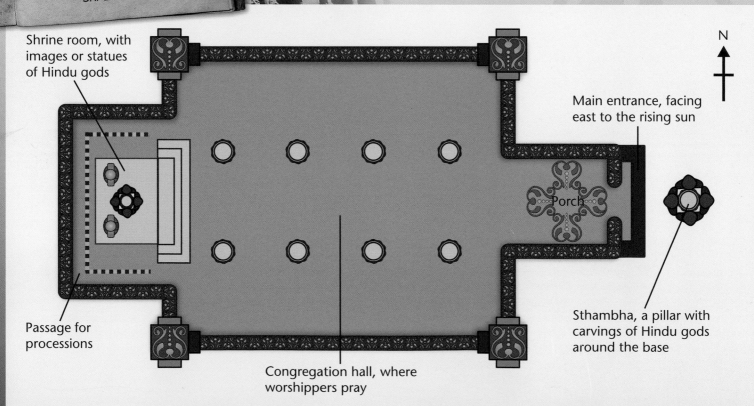

Shrine room, with images or statues of Hindu gods

N

Main entrance, facing east to the rising sun

Porch

Passage for processions

Sthambha, a pillar with carvings of Hindu gods around the base

Congregation hall, where worshippers pray

## Worshipping at Home

Hindus like to worship at home, often daily, and Hindu homes have a small shrine. The shrine is usually a small open cupboard, or a special room with a picture of the gods they worship. The family chants prayers, rings bells, and waves a candle before the shrine. Offerings of flowers, water, and clothes are made to the gods to invite them to come and live in the shrine. On special occasions, a priest comes to recite scriptures at the family shrine.

Offerings of flowers and water are made to the gods at a home shrine.

## Pilgrimages

Pilgrimages are journeys, especially long ones, made to sacred places. Hindus go on pilgrimages to places where the gods have been seen. Popular pilgrimage places include the Himalayas and certain temples and rivers. Rivers are very important to Hindus. They believe that if they bathe in a holy river, their **sins** are washed away.

When Hindus go on a pilgrimage they usually visit more than one place and may travel for some time. One Hindu pilgrimage route visits 108 places, believed to be places where the goddess Shakti was seen.

Pilgrims head to a holy river during Maha Kumbh Mela, a sacred pilgrimage and bathing festival in India.

Hindus immerse the Ganesha statue in the river after parading it through the streets.

# Festivals and Celebrations

Hindus celebrate several religious festivals throughout the year. Some can last for days, and involve presents and feasts. Two popular Hindu festivals are Lord Ganesha's birthday and Divali.

## Lord Ganesha's Birthday

Lord Ganesha is the elephant-headed son of the god, Shiva, and goddess, Parvati. Many Hindus believe that Shiva chopped off Ganesha's real head when he got angry with him, and replaced it with an elephant's head.

Ganesha is known as the Remover of Obstacles and his role is to help people to be brave and solve their problems. He also puts obstacles in people's way to stop them from going down the wrong path.

The festival celebrating Lord Ganesha's birthday occurs in August or September and lasts for ten days. Celebrations include:

- chanting with bells and clapping
- parades with musicians, singers, and acrobats
- making statues of Ganesha
- releasing a statue into the river.

## Divali

Divali (or Diwali) is also known as the Festival of Lights. It is a festival that symbolises good winning over evil.

There are several stories of different gods defeating evil creatures in Hinduism. This is why different Hindus celebrate and thank different gods during Divali. Some Hindus thank and pray to Lakshmi, the goddess of wealth, light, wisdom, and luck. They light lamps and ask Lakshmi to bless them and give them good luck for the next year.

To celebrate Divali, Hindus set off fireworks, put lamps up in their house, and share sweets. They wear new clothes, decorate their houses with flowers, have feasts, and give presents.

Divali is celebrated for five days in October or November and is a very happy time. It is also considered to be the beginning of the financial year in India. Shopkeepers settle up their accounts from the previous year and open new ones.

The Hindu calendar differs from the Western **Gregorian calendar**. Therefore, Hindu holy days fall on different dates each year. The dates in the Hindu calendar are forecast by astrologers one hundred years ahead. Here are some of the major Hindu celebrations:

**Shiva Ratri (Night of Lord Shiva)**

February or March

**Holi (Festival of Colors)**

Indian Hindus celebrate this two-day festival in late February or early March

**Ram Navmi (Lord Rama's Birthday)**

Nine-day festival in March or April

**Lord Ganesha's Birthday**

Ten-day festival in March or April

**Navratri (Festival of Goddesses)**

Nine-day festival in October

**Krishna's Birthday**

August or September

**Durga Puja (Goddess Durga Festival)**

Bengali Hindus celebrate this ten-day festival in September or October

**Divali (Festival of Lights)**

Five-day festival in October or November

A family celebrates Divali with flowers and candles in Karachi, Pakistan.

# Important Hindus

Due to the efforts of Ram Mohan Roy, sati was made illegal in 1829.

Two important Hindus who brought about change in India were Ram Mohan Roy and Mahatma Gandhi.

## Ram Mohan Roy 1772–1833 CE

Ram Mohan Roy was born in 1772 CE in India. He wanted to be a monk but his parents would not let him. They had married him to three wives by the time he was nine.

Ram Mohan studied Hindu scriptures and scriptures from other religions. He translated some into Bengali, Hindi and English so that more people could read them. He believed people should live simply, think deeply, and not worship **idols**. He also believed that everyone belongs to one family.

Ram Mohan campaigned to India's parliament to abolish the practice of sati. Sati was a Hindu funeral custom where a widow would leap onto her husband's **funeral pyre** and be burned to death. Ram Mohan saved many women from dying horrible deaths with his successful campaign against the practice.

Ram Mohan set up schools to help young people understand the Western world. He fought for freedom of the press and to stop children from being married. He also campaigned for women's rights to receive an education and to own property.

Ram Mohan Roy is often remembered as the "father of modern India."

# Mahatma Gandhi    1869–1948 CE

Mohandas Karamchand Gandhi was born in 1869 CE in India, when Britain was in charge of the country. He is commonly known as Mahatma, which means 'Great Soul'. Gandhi developed the idea of Satyagraha, which is fighting against unfair conditions peacefully and without violence. Gandhi was the political and spiritual leader of the Indian independence movement, and campaigned hard for independence from Britain.

Gandhi's Satyagraha, or non-cooperation, movement included:

- encouraging Indians to make and wear their own cloth instead of buying British-made textiles
- encouraging the boycott of British products, schools, law courts, and government
- the famous Salt March in 1930 to protest against the British salt tax. Gandhi marched for 249 miles (400 kilometers) to reach the sea to make salt himself, with thousands of Indians joining him along the way.

Gandhi also fought against the discrimination of different castes in India. He believed that there is one god present in all religions and wanted religious harmony between Hindus, Sikhs, and Muslims in India.

In 1948, Gandhi was shot and killed by a Hindu who felt he was too worried about Muslims. Gandhi's last word was "Rama," the Hindu god who represents a life of good behavior.

Gandhi's Satyagraha movement led to India's independence from Britain.

We must become the change we want to see in the world.

MAHATMA GANDHI

# Clothes and Food

As Hinduism began in India, India has a big influence on the type of clothes Hindus wear.

## Clothes for Women and Men

Hindu women usually wear a sari. This is a long piece of brightly colored material which is wound and pleated over the waist. Women wear an underskirt and a short blouse beneath the sari. One end of the sari is draped over the shoulder. Part of the tummy is sometimes shown, but the legs are covered.

Hindu men may wear normal pants with a long tunic. A traditional Hindu will wear loose pants and a jacket with buttons down the front and a special collar called a "Nehru" collar.

### Body Decoration

Hindu women wear a colored spot on their forehead, called a bindi. If they are married they wear a red bindi and if they are widowed or single, they may wear a black bindi. **Henna** patterns are also painted on women's hands, arms, and feet at weddings and on special occasions.

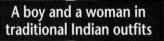
A boy and a woman in traditional Indian outfits

Wearing henna patterns as body art has been practiced in India for many centuries.

A sadhu, or holy man, makes a dinner of corn on the street.

# Food

Different Hindus have different beliefs about food. These beliefs include whether or not they should eat meat and which foods they believe can affect spirituality.

## Meat

Many Hindus do not eat any meat at all. Others eat some meat but never beef because the cow is a sacred animal. Most Hindus will not eat any food that may have caused pain to animals.

## Food that Affects Spirituality

Some Hindus believe that consuming alcohol, onions, and garlic makes it harder to find spiritual truths. They believe that dairy products such as milk, butter, and yogurt help with spirituality.

## Fasting

Some Hindus choose to **fast**. When some Hindus fast they eat and drink nothing. Others will drink water, but no other liquid or food. Hindus fast to make their favorite god happy or to give their food to someone who needs it more. Sharing food is an important Hindu custom. The scriptures say that Hindus should offer food to anyone who is hungry. It is a religious duty.

A typical Hindu meal is vegetarian.

# Birth

OM is a sacred symbol and sound in Hinduism.

In Hinduism, before a baby is born, special prayers are said for the mother. The prayers are that she and the baby will be healthy, and that the baby will be intelligent, loving, and have an advanced **soul**.

When the baby is born, the father draws the sacred **OM** symbol on the baby's tongue using a gold pen dipped in honey and **ghee**. He also recites sacred verses to make the baby more intelligent.

## Horoscopes

The exact time, date, and place of birth is written down. Later, a priest will use the time of the birth to draw up a **horoscope** for the baby. Hindus believe that **astrology** has a big influence on their lives.

In astrology, there are twelve star signs.

## Naming Ceremony

At least twelve days after the baby is born, there is a naming ceremony. The baby's name is often influenced by the baby's horoscope. The naming ceremony may take place in front of a sacred fire. The naming ceremony may also be performed at home.

The naming ceremony can include:

- dressing the baby in special clothes
- whispering the baby's name into their ear
- saying special prayers
- tying a yellow thread around the baby's waist
- laying the baby on a banana leaf or a sheet.

There are other rituals for the baby as they get older. These include the first time they are given solid food and the first time they go outside.

This Hindu baby is wrapped in red cloth for the naming ceremony.

# Growing Up

Two ceremonies for young Hindus growing up are the Ritu Kala ceremony for girls and Upanayana ceremony for boys.

## Ritu Kala

When girls reach puberty, a Ritu Kala ceremony may be organized at their home. However, the ceremony is not performed very often.

Ritu Kala celebrates the physical and emotional changes the girl is experiencing. Usually only women are present and during the ceremony the girl may receive her first sari. The women sing songs of praise, put powder on her forehead, neck and arms, and give her gifts and blessings.

Ritu Kala gifts may include new clothes, fruit, flowers, jewelry, gold, silver, and silks. Sometimes girls receive green-colored gifts to welcome their new fertility. After the ceremony there is a big feast.

The Ritu Kala ceremony is performed when young girls reach puberty.

## Upanayana

Upanayana, the sacred thread ceremony, is for boys aged between seven and thirteen from the three highest castes. The boy receives three threads made of nine twisted strands. The three threads are tied together with a special knot.

The threads are to remind the boy he has three debts to pay:

- a debt to God
- a debt to his parents and ancestors
- a debt to the wise people of his religion.

The thread is usually draped over the boy's left shoulder and down to the right hip, and can be worn for the rest of his life. A priest conducts the ceremony and the boy's father recites prayers.

After receiving the three threads, the boy can now study Sanskrit, which is the language of the Hindu scriptures. He must also pray three times a day, study sacred writings, and perform some religious ceremonies.

A bride has her hair done and her hands painted with henna in preparation for her wedding.

# Marriage

There are many Hindu traditions when choosing a partner and getting married.

## Choosing a Partner

Many Hindu marriages are still arranged by the parents. Hindus believe that parents know their children best and will know who would make the best partner for them. Whether the parents or they themselves choose their partner, a priest will always check the couples' horoscopes to make sure they are a good match.

## Wedding Clothes

At the wedding, the bride may wear a red sari, or a red and white sari with gold thread. She wears jewelry, body decoration, herbs, and henna oil. The groom wears a scarf draped over his shoulder. He may wear a long white, ivory, or beige tunic embroidered with gold thread and a turban with a veil of flowers.

The bride and groom often wear garlands of flowers for the ceremony. Flowers represent happiness and good luck.

The sacred wedding fire is an important part of a Hindu wedding ceremony.

## Wedding Ceremony

There are many rituals in a Hindu wedding ceremony. One is that the priest builds a sacred wedding fire. The bride and groom circle the fire seven times, stopping to touch a stone in their path with their toes. This is to symbolise that they will overcome life's obstacles together.

In another ritual, the bride's sari and the groom's scarf are tied together. This sacred knot symbolizes that the marriage is for always. The couple then take seven steps together to represent the important things in married life:

1 healthy food
2 physical, mental, and spiritual strength
3 wealth
4 knowledge and love
5 children
6 self-control and a long life
7 friendship and companionship.

# Death and the Afterlife

Pallbearers, carrying the body, lead a funeral procession through the streets of Pashupatinah in Nepal.

*H*indus believe that when they die they should be **cremated**. They also believe in reincarnation.

## The Funeral

Hindus believe families can help a person's next life by supporting them as they are dying. Relatives chant parts of the Vedas or sing hymns around the dying person so that their last thoughts are about Brahman. Thinking about Brahman as they die improves the chances of a good reincarnation.

After a person dies the relatives gather around them and pray. The body is washed and then dressed, usually in white. If a woman dies before her husband she may be dressed in red bridal clothes. The body is decorated with flowers and sandalwood. Scriptures are read and then the eldest son lights the funeral pyre, circles the body, and prays for the departing soul.

Hindus are cremated when they die because they believe it helps the soul to leave the body faster. After the cremation, the family may have a meal together and pray in their home. A priest will visit their house to purify it with spices and incense.

## Life After Death

According to Hinduism, after a person dies they may be reborn. If they have led a bad life they may come back as a person who will have a lot of problems, or even as an animal. If they have led a good life, they may come back as a priest. If they have led a very, very good and holy life, they will not be born again but will become part of Brahman.

One year after a person's death, the family gives money to the poor in memory of their dead relative. Most Hindu families pray each year during September or October in memory of their **ancestors**. This time is called the Pitra Pakch, which means Prayer for Ancestors.

Brothers of an Indian Hindu family pray for their ancestors in Mumbai, in India.

# Hinduism Around the World

*H*induism is the world's third-largest religion. There are about 900 million Hindus worldwide. The majority of Hindus live in India. In fact, 81 percent of India's population are Hindus. In Mauritius, 48 percent of the people are Hindus and Nepal is the world's only official Hindu state.

There are also Hindus in Guyana, Fiji, Bhutan, Bangladesh, Malaysia, Myanmar (Burma), Singapore, Sri Lanka, Suriname, Trinidad and Tobago, Britain, Indonesia, Japan, Thailand, Africa, the United States, Canada, New Zealand, and Australia.

**This map shows the top ten Hindu countries.**

ARCTIC OCEAN

ARCTIC OCEAN

**NEPAL**
**81 percent**

**BHUTAN**
**25 percent**

**INDIA**
**81 percent**

ATLANTIC OCEAN

PACIFIC OCEAN

**TRINIDAD AND TOBAGO**
**23 percent**

**BANGLADESH**
**16 percent**

PACIFIC OCEAN

**GUYANA**
**35 percent**

**SRI LANKA**
**7 percent**

**SURINAME**
**27 percent**

**MAURITIUS**
**48 percent**

**FIJI**
**34 percent**

INDIAN OCEAN

N
W  E
S

**KEY**

| | |
|---|---|
| | area of country |
| **NEPAL** | name of country |
| **81 percent** | percentage of country population that is Hindu |

SOUTHERN OCEAN

SOUTHERN OCEAN

# Glossary

| | |
|---|---|
| ancestors | members of a family who lived a long time ago |
| astrology | the study of the positions of the stars and planets in the belief that they have an influence over people's lives |
| Brahman | the divine and sacred power that is the source of all existence |
| cremated | burning a dead body until only ashes are left |
| faith | belief in the teachings of a religion |
| fast | to not eat, or eat very little |
| funeral pyre | pile of wood for burning a dead body at a funeral ceremony |
| ghee | a type of butter used especially in Indian cooking |
| Gregorian calendar | the most widely used calendar in the world, based on the cycle of the Sun |
| henna | a reddish-orange dye made from the leaves of the henna plant |
| horoscope | prediction of someone's future based on studying the positions of the planets and stars |
| idols | images used as objects of worship |
| karma | the principle that a person's actions in this life determine their destiny in the next life |
| mantras | sacred verses from the Vedas chanted over and over again |
| moksha | to be released from the cycle of rebirth and become one with Brahman |
| OM | the most sacred sound and symbol in Sanskrit, used to represent Brahman, as a mantra, and in blessings |
| orally | spoken rather than written |
| pilgrimages | journeys, often long ones, made to sacred places or temples |
| reincarnated | reborn in another body or form after death |
| scriptures | sacred writings |
| sins | bad actions, wrongs |
| soul | a person's spirit, which lives forever |

# Index